Kids' COOKBOOK

igloo

D0771013

Published by Igloo Books Limited
Garrard Way
Kettering
Northants
NN16 8TD
www.igloo-books.com

First published 2005
This edition published 2006

The publisher, author, and editor have made every reasonable effort to
ensure that the recipes in this book are safe when made as instructed
but assume no responsibility for any damage caused or sustained while
making recipes in this book. Parents, guardians, and/or teachers should
supervise young readers who cook the recipes in this book.

Some recipes in this book contain nuts.

ISBN 1-84561-107-1

Project management Kandour

Editorial and design management: Emma Hayley and Jenny Ross
Author: James Mitchell
Design and layout: Kurt Young
Cover design: Paul Barton
Editor: Josephine Bacon
Photography: CEPHAS / StockFood;
CEPHAS / Vince Hart (page 32); Photos.com

Contents

Before you start

Cooking is great fun but, with lots of hot and sharp things around, it can also be dangerous. Make sure you read these simple rules and follow them every time you are in the kitchen, so as to be safe, and the food you cook will be delicious.

The Rules

1 NEVER COOK ANYTHING WITHOUT AN ADULT THERE TO HELP YOU.

2 Always ask a grown-up to help you with anything sharp, hot or electrical, and don't be afraid to ask questions, even the best chefs ask for help.

3 Before you start cooking, always give your hands a good wash with soap and clean the work surfaces.

4 When you're using a knife, be very careful and always use a chopping board. Hold the knife firmly, point the blade downwards, and keep your fingers out of the way.

5 Whenever you need to move something hot, always use oven gloves or a pot-holder. Anything hot can give you a nasty burn, so it's better to get a grown-up to handle the hot stuff for you. If you burn yourself, run the cold tap and hold the burn under it straight away and continue for at least 10 minutes. It will feel really, really cold, but it's worth it because the burn won't sting later.

6 Make sure the handles of saucepans aren't sticking out from the cooker or work surface so no one can knock against them. That goes for the grown-ups too!

7 Make sure your hands are dry before you touch anything electrical, such as plugs, sockets and blenders. If your hands are wet, you could give yourself an electric shock.

8 Keep a clean cloth nearby and wipe up anything you spill straight away, especially if it's on the floor.

9 Hot pots and pans should always be placed on a heat-proof mat or stand.

10 Bacteria are everywhere and sometimes food can have some on it that might make you ill. Always wash fruit and vegetables before you use them and wash your hands, knife and chopping board when you've been touching raw fish or meat. Always clean up and tidy up as you work.

Watch out for:

The measurements are given here in metric and imperial measures. It is very important to stick to one type of measurement only in any recipe.

11 **Making sure your food tastes great!** Read the recipe all the way through before you shop for the ingredients and before you start cooking. Make a shopping list, then get a grown-up to check it for you, because you might have some of the ingredients already.

12 Take extra care weighing and measuring ingredients. If you rush this, it's easy for your recipe to go wrong. Make sure you have a set of measuring spoons and kitchen scales too.

13 Don't rush, it's better for the food to be a little late than for it not to taste good. If you put love and care into your cooking it actually makes the food taste better!

14 **Finally the most important rule of all — HAVE FUN!!**

lb means pound
oz means ounce
fl oz means fluid ounce
g means gram
pt means pint
in means inch
cm means centimetre

Peanut Butter & Banana Wakey-shakey

Makes 1 Wakey-shakey

This is a quick milkshake for your breakfast. It will give you loads of energy for the morning!

You will need:
A blender

Ingredients

1 banana

1 heaped tablespoon smooth peanut butter

150ml/5fl oz milk

To decorate (optional):
Whipped cream and glacé cherries

1 Before you go to bed, peel and chop the banana into bite-size pieces.

2 Put it in a plastic bag and pop it in the freezer overnight.

3 When you wake up, put all the ingredients in the blender, get a grown-up to help you with this, and whizz it up for about a minute, until it's really thick and smooth. Make sure you hold the lid down when you switch on the blender or your shake might end up all over the kitchen!!

Extras!
Try swapping the peanut butter for one of these:

50g/2oz strawberries, blueberries or raspberries and a teaspoon of runny honey

1 heaped tablespoon of chocolate powder

Scrambles

Feeds 1

This is a really easy recipe that everyone likes!

You'll need:
A small mixing bowl
A toaster
A non-stick saucepan
A wooden spoon

Ingredients

2 free-range eggs

2 slices of bread

A pinch of salt

100g/4oz butter

To decorate (optional):
Chopped chives

Extras!
For something a bit more special,
try adding:
- 50g/2oz grated cheese with 50g/2oz chopped ham
- 50g/2oz of chopped smoked salmon
- One hot dog sausage, chopped.

Just add any of these to the eggs when you turn off the
heat and give it all a good stir with the wooden spoon.

1 Crack the eggs into a bowl, add the salt and beat with a fork.

2 Next, put the bread in the toaster ready to toast.

3 Heat 15g/^{1}/2oz of the butter in the saucepan over a medium heat. When the butter has melted, press the bread down in the toaster. Then pour the beaten eggs into the melted butter and start stirring them with a wooden spoon. The secret of good scrambled eggs is to keep mixing the eggs all the time and to make sure you get the spoon right into the corners and edges of the pan, mixing in any bits that are sticking.

4 When the eggs are creamy and still slightly runny, turn off the heat. They'll keep cooking by themselves for a little longer.

5 Butter your toast, which should have popped up by now, and either serve the eggs on top of it or on the side.

Cinnamon French Toast

Feeds 1

Sweet and tangy, this is a great alternative to plain old toast!

You'll need:
A small mixing bowl
A non-stick frying pan
A fish slice
Oven gloves
An apron

Ingredients

1 free-range egg

150ml/5fl oz milk

2 tablespoons brown sugar

2 teaspoons powdered cinnamon

2 thick slices white bread

Butter for frying

1 Break the egg into the bowl. Add the milk, sugar, and cinnamon, and beat with the fork until it's well mixed.

2 Next, soak the bread slices in the egg mixture. Make sure they are completely covered.

3 Put on your oven gloves and apron. Get a grown-up to help you heat your frying pan to a medium heat and add a knob of butter. When the butter has melted and has started to foam, add in your soaked bread and fry until it is golden-brown underneath. You can check this by carefully lifting up the end with the fish slice. Flip the bread slices over with the fish slice and fry them on the other side.

Extras!
Try regular French toast, which is also yummy. Just don't add the sugar and cinnamon, and then serve it with a couple of rashers of bacon or baked beans. You can also add strips of orange zest to the egg mixture, as in the picture.

Pancake Pals

Makes 4 pancake pals

This recipe is great for you to make for the family at the weekends or if you have friends to sleep over!

You'll need:
A blender
A fish slice
A ladle
An apron
A non-stick frying pan

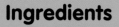

Ingredients

200g/8oz plain flour

3 teaspoons baking powder

A pinch of salt

2 teaspoons vegetable oil plus extra for frying

375ml/13fl oz milk

2 free-range eggs

12 blueberries

2 strawberries, cut in half

Maple syrup for serving

1 First preheat the oven to the lowest setting.

2 Put on your apron and get a grown-up to help you with this. Using electrical appliances and cooking can be dangerous as the frying pan and oil will be very hot, so never try this on your own.

3 Put everything apart from the blueberries, strawberries and maple syrup in the blender. Put on the lid, and whizz it all for a minute until it's all mixed up and smooth. Don't forget to hold on the lid before you switch on the blender or you'll be wearing your breakfast!!

4 Heat up the frying pan to a medium heat and add half a teaspoon of the oil, then pour a ladle of pancake mix into the middle of the frying pan for the face and then pour two little bits on for the ears. When bubbles start to appear in the middle of your pancake, flip it over with the fish slice and cook for another minute, or until both sides are golden-brown.

5 Put the pancake on a plate and ask a grown-up to put it in the oven while you make the rest.

6 When you've cooked the 4 pancakes, put them on plates and decorate them. Add half a strawberry for the mouth and blueberries for the eyes and nose.

7 Serve with the maple syrup poured round the edge.

Extras!
Try adding 100g/4oz of blueberries to the pancake mix before frying them, or serve each pancake with two rashers of grilled bacon.

Oatmeal and Fruit Breakfast

Makes 2 servings

This is good because you do all the hard work before bedtime and when you're sleepy in the morning your yummy breakfast is already made!!

You'll need:
A medium mixing bowl
A cheese grater

Ingredients

150g/5oz porridge oats

1 green eating apple

150ml/5fl oz
plain yogurt

75ml/3fl oz milk

2 teaspoons runny
honey or maple syrup

1 Put the oats, milk, yogurt and honey in the mixing bowl.

2 Next cut the apple into quarters and the cut out the core. Then grate the apple, without peeling it and mix it into the mixing bowl before it turns brown. Give it all a really good stir and then cover it with some clingfilm and refrigerate it ready for the morning.

3 When you wake up in the morning, share the mixture between two bowls, and then choose two or three of the following ingredients to put into each bowl:
25g/1oz chopped nuts
25g/1oz currants, raisins or any other dried fruits
25g/1oz raspberries, blueberries or chopped up strawberries
$1/2$ chopped up banana, 25g/1oz apples shaped like stars, and pieces of chopped orange.

Cornflake Muffins

Makes 12

These are nice at anytime of the day, but they're great for a quick breakfast when you're late for school.

You'll need

A large mixing bowl
A wooden spoon
A 12-cup muffin pan

Ingredients

100g/4oz porridge oats

300ml/^{1}/2pt milk

A little butter

1 free-range egg

125ml/4fl oz vegetable oil

175g/6oz brown sugar

50g/2oz cornflakes

150g/5oz raisins

150g/5oz dried
    apricots, chopped

150g/5oz plain flour

4 teaspoons baking powder

1 teaspoon salt

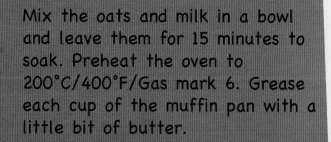

1 Mix the oats and milk in a bowl and leave them for 15 minutes to soak. Preheat the oven to 200°C/400°F/Gas mark 6. Grease each cup of the muffin pan with a little bit of butter.

2 Beat the egg, oil, three-quarters of the brown sugar, half the cornflakes, and all of the raisins, and the apricots into the oat and milk mixture.

3 Next beat in the flour, baking powder and salt into the mixture Divide the mixture between the cups of the muffin pan and sprinkle the tops with the rest of the cornflakes and brown sugar.

4 Get a grown-up to bake them in the oven for 20 to 25 minutes, or until they've puffed up and are golden-brown.

5 They'll keep in an air-tight container for about a week.

Extras!
Try swapping the raisins and apricots for the same amount of other dried fruit, such as dried cranberries, blueberries or dates. You can even add chocolate chips.

Gingerbread People

Makes 15 to 20 people

"Run, run as fast as you can! You can't catch me
I'm the Gingerbread Man!"

You'll need:
A sieve
A large mixing bowl
A saucepan
A wooden spoon
A rolling pin
Gingerbread people
 cookie cutters
A baking tray
A palette knife
A wire cooling rack
A piping bag or a
 plastic freezer bag

Ingredients

225g/8oz plain flour
1 teaspoon baking powder
2 teaspoons ground ginger
100g/4oz butter, softened
75g/3oz soft brown sugar
2 tablespoons golden syrup

To decorate (optional):
100g/4oz icing sugar;
currants or pieces of
glacé cherries

1 Preheat the oven to 180°C/350°F/Gas mark 4. Sift the flour, baking powder and ginger into a mixing bowl.

2 Ask a grown-up to melt the butter, sugar and golden syrup in a saucepan. Let the mixture cool for a few minutes and then pour into the flour mixture. Stir it with a wooden spoon and then knead it into a big ball with you hands.

3 Dust a work surface and rolling pin with a little flour and then roll the dough out until it's about $1/2$cm/$1/4$in thick. Use the cookie cutter to cut out the people. If you have any dough left, roll it out again and cut out a couple more.

4 Transfer the people to a baking tray with a palette knife. Ask a grown-up to bake them in the middle of the oven for 10 to 12 minutes until they are golden-brown.

5 Let them cool down for a few minutes and then move them to a wire rack to cool.

6 For the icing, sift the icing sugar into a bowl, add a tablespoon of water, and mix it together. Spoon it into a piping bag or a freezer bag with the tip of a corner snipped off, and draw faces and clothes on your people.

7 You can push currants or little pieces of glacé cherries into your cookies for eyes and buttons.

Squidgy Chocolate Brownies

Makes 12-15 brownies

These lovely chocolate brownies are chewy and squidgy in the middle!

You'll need:

A 20cm/8in square baking tin
A microwave oven or a
   large saucepan
A large mixing bowl
A wooden spoon
A sieve
A palette knife
Oven gloves
A wire cooling rack

Ingredients:

Extra butter for greasing
   the tin
50g/2oz dark
   baking chocolate
100g/4oz butter, softened
1 teaspoon vanilla essence
225g/8oz sugar
2 free-range eggs
50g/2oz plain flour
1/2 teaspoon baking powder
A pinch of salt

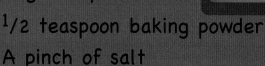

1 Preheat the oven to: 180°C/350°F/Gas mark 4 and grease the baking tin with a little butter.

2 Break up the chocolate and put it in the mixing bowl. Microwave it for 2 minutes on the defrost setting or until it has all melted. If you don't have a microwave, get a grown-up to heat about 5cm/2in water in a large saucepan until it's steaming and then put the mixing bowl on top to melt the chocolate.

3 Next mix in the butter, vanilla essence and sugar into the melted chocolate, beating with a wooden spoon. When the mixture is smooth, beat the eggs and stir them in. Sift the flour, salt and baking powder into the bowl and beat the mixture until smooth. Pour the mixture into the greased baking tin and spread it out to the corners, using the palette knife.

Extras!
Try adding 50g/2oz chocolate chips, raisins or chopped nuts to the mixture at stage 3.

4 Get a grown-up to put the tin in the middle of the oven and bake the mixture for 25 to 30 minutes, or until the edges are firm, but the cake is springy in the middle.

5 Let the tin cool down for 15 minutes then cut the cake into 12 to 15 squares using the palette knife. Arrange the brownies on the wire cooling rack and leave them to cool.

Chocolate Crackles

Everyone loves these crunchy little chocolate treats. Make sure you keep them away from the grown-ups!

You'll need:

A mixing bowl

Microwave oven or a large saucepan

A wooden spoon

15 paper cupcake cases

Ingredients

150g/5oz chocolate (milk, white, or dark, whichever you like best)

1 tablespoon runny honey

50g/2oz butter

150g/5oz cornflakes

Extras!

Try using different types of breakfast cereal, such as Rice Crispies or add 50g/2oz raisins or chopped nuts to the chocolate.

1 Break the chocolate into pieces. The easy way to do this is to tap the packet sharply on the edge of the work surface before you open it. Next put the chocolate, honey and butter in the mixing bowl.

2 Put the bowl in the microwave oven on the defrost setting and cook for 2 minutes, or until the chocolate has melted.

3 If you don't have a microwave oven, get a grown-up to heat about 5cm/2in water in a large saucepan until it's steaming, then put the mixing bowl on top to melt the chocolate.

4 Stir the mixture with a wooden spoon until it's smooth and then carefully stir in the cornflakes so they are completely covered with the melted chocolate.

5 Spoon a tablespoon of the mixture into each of the paper cupcake cases, leave to cool to room temperature, and then put them in the refrigerator to set.

Fruity Frozen Yogurt

Makes 14-16 servings

This is an easy way to make a tasty and healthy version of ice-cream.

You'll need:
A food processor
A mixing bowl
A plastic ice-cream tub
An ice-cream maker
or a wooden spoon

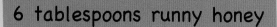

Ingredients

700g/1lb 9oz fresh or frozen berries (raspberries, strawberries, blueberries whichever is you favourite)

6 tablespoons runny honey

1.1litres/2pt plain yogurt

1 Put everything in a food processor and process until it's smooth. Get a grown-up to help you with this as food processors can be dangerous.

2 If you've got an ice-cream maker, get a grown-up to show you how to use it as they all work differently.

3 If you don't have an ice-cream maker, pour the mixture into a plastic ice cream tub, cover it, and put in the freezer. After an hour, take it out of the freezer and give it a really good mix with a wooden spoon. This breaks up the ice crystals and makes it smoother and creamier.

4 Do this once or twice more. The yogurt will keep in the freezer for several weeks, if you don't finish it off before!!!

Extras!
Serve your fruity frozen yogurt with toppings, such as fresh berries (the same or different ones from the ones you put in the frozen yogurt), sprinkles or chopped nuts.

Peanut Butter Cookies

Makes about 36 cookies

These peanut butter cookies are great to share. Why not take some to school to share with your friends?

You'll need:

A large mixing bowl
A wooden spoon
A fork
A sieve
A large non-stick
   or greased baking sheet
Oven gloves
A wire cooling rack

Ingredients

150g/5oz soft butter

150g/5oz smooth
   peanut butter

1 teaspoon vanilla essence

225g/8oz soft
   brown sugar

2 free-range eggs

200g/8oz plain flour

1 teaspoon baking powder

1/2 teaspoon salt

1 Preheat the oven to:
180°C/350°F/Gas Mark 4.

2 Put the butter, peanut butter, vanilla essence and sugar into the mixing bowl and beat together. Next, beat the eggs with a fork and then beat them into the mixture.

3 Sift the flour, baking powder and salt into the peanut butter mixture, and mix together until the mixture is smooth.

4 Drop tablespoons of the mixture on to the baking sheet. You don't have to spread them out. Then get a grown-up to put them in the oven for you. Bake them for 10 minutes if you like them chewy, or for 15 minutes if you like them crispy.

5 Let the cookies cool on the baking sheet for 5 minutes and then move them to a wire rack to cool down completely.

Extras!

Trying adding 100g/4oz chopped raw peanuts or chocolate chips to the mixture, or arrange peanuts and chocolate on the top of the cookies to look like faces.

Choc Chip Cookies

Makes 16-20

Choc chip cookies are great with a glass of milk.

You'll need:

A mixing bowl
A wooden spoon
A teaspoon
A tablespoon
2 baking sheets
A wire cooling rack
Oven gloves

Ingredients

100g/4oz softened butter

75g/3oz soft brown sugar

75g/3oz caster sugar

1 free-range egg

1/2 teaspoon baking
   powder

1/2 teaspoon vanilla
   essence

225g/8oz plain flour

150g/5oz milk
chocolate chips

Extra butter for greasing
the baking sheets

1 Preheat the oven to:
180°C/350°F/Gas mark 4.

2 Put the butter and sugars into a bowl and beat together until the mixture is creamy.

3 Then break the egg into the bowl, add the baking powder and vanilla essence, and beat into the mixture until smooth.

4 Now stir in the flour a little at a time so it's well mixed, then stir in the chocolate chips.

5 Rub a little butter over the baking sheets so the cookies don't stick, then put teaspoonfuls of the mixture on the sheets, making sure there is plenty of room between each one because the cookies will spread out during baking.

6 Get a grown-up to put them in the oven for you and bake for about 12 to 15 minutes. The cookies should be golden and firm.

7 Leave them to cool for 5 minutes and then put them on the wire rack to cool down completely.

Extras!

For double-choc cookies, add 2 tablespoons unsweetened cocoa powder to the mixture when you add the flour. For treble-choc cookies add the cocoa plus 75g/3oz white chocolate chips! You could also try adding 100g/4oz chopped nuts for choc nut cookies.

Banana Split

Makes 1

Banana Split has been eaten for years and everyone still loves it!

You'll need:
A plastic knife
An ice-cream scoop

Ingredients

1 banana

2 scoops ice-cream or frozen yogurt

Toppings:

Chocolate, raspberry or strawberry sauce

Strawberries, raspberries, blueberries, cherries or grapes

Chopped nuts, sprinkles or chocolate chips

1 Peel the banana and then slice it down the middle lengthways. Arrange the banana in a sundae glass and put 2 scoops of ice-cream on top of it.

2 Cover your banana split with lots of toppings!

Icy Poles

Why spend lots of money on ice lollies at the shop when you can make nicer ones at home? You can buy really inexpensive lolly-making kits from cookware shops. Why not save up your pocket money and buy a set, you'll make great savings in the long run!

You'll need:
A set of ice lolly moulds

Ingredients

Juices: Orange, apple, grape, pineapple, cranberry or a mixture.
Smoothies: Strawberry, mango, blueberry.
Cordial: Blackcurrant, orange, lemon.
Fizzy drinks: Lemonade, cola, cream soda.

1 This is so easy you could do it with you eyes closed! All you need to do is fill up the moulds with your favourite drinks and put them in the freezer until they are completely frozen. Be careful to pour any fizzy drink slowly, as it will fizz up!

Flapjacks

Makes about 10 chewy flapjacks

You'll need:
A mixing bowl
A wooden spoon
A shallow 20cm/8in square baking tin
Oven gloves
Apron

Ingredients

100g/4oz butter

50g/2oz soft brown sugar

4 tablespoons golden syrup

250g/9oz rolled or porridge oats

1 Preheat oven to: 180°C/350°F/Gas mark 4. Butter the baking tin.

2 Put the butter, sugar and golden syrup into a saucepan. With a grown-up to help you, stir the sauce over a low heat until the butter has melted and the sugar has dissolved.

3 Next add the oats to the pan, and stir well. Pour the mixture into the tin, pressing it down firmly until it is about 5cm/2in thick.

4 Get a grown-up to put the flapjacks in the oven and bake for 20 to 25 minutes, or until golden.

5 Ask a grown-up to take them out of the oven. Leave them to cool for 15 minutes in the tin, then cut into squares or rectangles.

Extras!
Why not try adding 2 tablespoons currants or a teaspoon ground ginger?

Sticky Chicken Wings

Feeds 4

The best food is stuff you can eat with your fingers.
These are great for a snack or as fun party food!

You'll need:
A mixing bowl
A fork
A baking tray
Oven gloves
Kitchen tongs

Ingredients

2 tablespoons olive or sunflower oil

2 tablespoons fresh orange juice

2 tablespoons soy sauce

2 tablespoons runny honey

1/2 teaspoon smoked paprika

1 garlic clove, crushed

12 chicken wings

1 Put everything apart from the chicken wings in a bowl and mix them together with a fork.

2 Then add the chicken wings and stir them around until they are completely coated in the sauce. Cover the bowl with clingfilm and refrigerate it for 1 to 2 hours, to marinate. That means all the flavours will get into the chicken.

3 Preheat the oven 200°C/400°F/Gas mark 6.

4 Put the wings on a baking tray and pour the rest of the sauce over them. Get a grown-up to put them in the middle of the oven to bake for 15 minutes.

5 After 15 minutes, get a grown-up to take them out of the oven and turn them over with a pair of tongs. If you're careful, you can help with this, but make sure you're with a grown-up and watch out for the hot baking tray!

6 Then put them back in the oven for another 15 minutes.

7 When they are ready, make sure you've got lots of paper towels to wipe your sticky fingers!

Extras!

Try swapping the honey for maple syrup. Also, when your turning over the wings after 15 minutes, try sprinkling them with 2 tablespoons sesame seeds to coat them all over.

Garlic Bread

Makes 1 loaf

Eating lots of garlic can make your breath smell a bit the next day, so makes sure that everyone eats some and then none of you will notice!

You'll need:
A garlic press
A serrated plastic knife
A chopping board
A butter knife
A small bowl
Some aluminium foil
Oven gloves

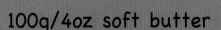

Ingredients

1 French baguette

100g/4oz soft butter

4 cloves of garlic, crushed

1/2 teaspoon salt

1 Preheat the oven to: 180°C/350°F/Gas mark 4.

2 Mix together the garlic, butter and salt in the bowl.

3 Now put the baguette on the chopping board and get a grown-up to help you cut into it with a plastic knife. The slices should be about 2.5cm/1in wide, but stop about 1.5cm/^{1}/2in from the bottom so the baguette is still joined up.

4 Use the butter knife to spread the garlic butter between all of the cuts and then push the baguette back together again.

5 Wrap the baguette loosely in aluminium foil, scrunching the ends together so it's sealed up. Then get a grown-up to put it in the oven, where it should bake for 25 minutes.

6 When a grown-up has taken it out of the oven, let it cool down for 2 minutes then carefully unwrap the aluminium foil, because it will be very hot inside. Now it's ready to eat!

Extras!

For cheesy garlic bread, try pushing 100g/4oz grated Cheddar cheese into the cuts before baking the bread. Or for herby garlic bread, try mixing a tablespoon of freshly chopped herbs such as rosemary, parsley or thyme into the butter.

Quesadillas (Kes-sah-dee-ahhhs!)

Makes 4

These quesadillas are a really quick and tasty snack you can make for your friends after school or when you've been out playing.

You'll need:

A cheese grater
A serrated plastic knife
A chopping board
A spoon
A mixing bowl
Oven gloves

Ingredients

150g/4oz Cheddar cheese, grated

1/2 red onion, finely chopped

1 sweet red pepper, finely chopped

220g/7oz can mixed beans, drained

220g/7oz can of sweetcorn, drained

4 x 30cm/12in flour tortillas

1 Get a grown-up to grate the cheese, using the cheese grater. Watch the sharp bits on the grater!

2 Carefully peel and finely chop the onion with a plastic knife on the chopping board. Cut the red pepper in half and scrape out the seeds and white bits with a spoon. Chop the flesh into small squares.

3 Get a grown-up to open the cans of beans and sweetcorn and drain them. Then put them in a mixing bowl with the cheese, pepper and onion, and mix together.

4 Spread your mixture over two of the four tortillas then fold the other two over them to make a sandwich.

5 Get a grown-up to heat up the grill, and grill the quesadillas for 2 to 3 minutes on each side so they are golden-brown. Then diagonally slice each quesadilla into three pieces. Start munching!

Extras!
You can try adding one or two of these to the mixture:
150g/4oz chopped ham or chopped, cooked chicken
2 chopped tomatoes
4 chopped mushrooms
or 2 tablespoons chopped fresh coriander leaves

Smiley Sandwiches

Makes 2

These are like paintings that you can eat and you can make them different every time. The faces can be decorated with any ingredients you have in the kitchen, just check with a grown-up before you use them.

Ingredients

6 tablespoon cottage cheese

2 slices of bread

Mustard cress or alfalfa

Paprika

2 baby radishes, sliced

Salsa

Strips and slices of cucumber

Sweet pepper, sliced

Spread the cottage cheese over the slices of bread

2 Sprinkle some cress or alfalfa at the top of the slice for hair and dust a little paprika across the middle for red cheeks.

3 For the eyes, use two slices of radish with a dot of salsa in the middle, then for eyebrows use two strips of cucumber. For the nose, use a little triangle of cucumber and for the mouth a slice of sweet pepper.

Snake Stick

Feeds 6

This is an exsssellent sssssnack to make for friendsssssss!

You'll need:
A serrated plastic knife
A chopping board
A butter knife
2 cocktail sticks

Ingredients

1 red pepper

1 baguette

Butter

12 slices salami
  or pepperoni

A few lettuce leaves,
  shredded

2 olives (stuffed
  with red pepper)

Tomato ketchup

Extras!
You can try filling your snake with other
ingredients. Slices of cheese, ham, cucumber,
tomato – anything you want!

1 Cut the pepper in half and scrape out the seeds and white parts with a spoon. Then slice it, saving a strip for the tongue. To make the tongue, just cut a V in one end.

2 Next, cut the baguette in half lengthways through the centre and butter the lower half, using the butter knife. Layer the strips of pepper over the butter, then add layers of salami and lettuce. Finally, put the top half of the baguette over the lower half, and push down firmly.

3 Next, to make the face of your snake, poke the tongue out of one end of the baguette, and stick on the olives with the cocktail sticks for its eyes.

4 Chop the baguette into sections and arrange the pieces in an S-shape like a wiggly snake. To make its markings, squeeze a zigzag strip of tomato ketchup along its back.

Have fun with veg!

Try having fun with vegetables. Take a serrated plastic knife and chop, carve and shape vegetables into various cute animals and items. Use a cocktail stick and cream cheese to stick bits together. It's like an art class in the kitchen!

Stringy Nachos

This is a super-quick snack to make when you're hungry

You'll need:
A plastic serrated knife
A spoon
A chopping board
A cheese grater

Ingredients

1 sweet red pepper

10 slices of jalapeño
  pepper (if you like it hot!!)

10 black olives, stoned

150g/5oz Cheddar or
  mozzarella cheese

1 packet tortilla chips

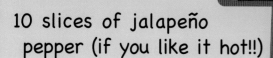

Extras!
Try putting other things on top of the tortilla chips, such as chopped tomato, thinly sliced red onion or chunks of avocado. If you've got some salsa or guacamole in the refrigerator you can put that on top too.

1 Preheat the grill to high. Cut the red pepper in half and scrape out the seeds and white bits with a spoon, then chop them into small pieces. Mix up with the jalapeño slices – make sure you wash your hands after this, and don't touch your eyes because otherwise the and jalapeño will make them sting! Then slice up the olives.

2 Get a grown-up to grate the cheese coarsely, using the large holes on the cheese grater. Be careful with the sharp bits! Sprinkle the tortilla chips over a large plate, then sprinkle with the olives and peppers, and finally with the cheese.

3 Get a grown-up to put the plate under the grill, and grill until the cheese has melted. You're done! Be careful with the plate though as it will be really hot.

Snack on a Stick

Feeds 4

Snacks you can eat on the move.

You'll need:
A plastic serrated knife
A spoon
A chopping board
Some wooden skewers

Ingredients

1 yellow sweet pepper

1 red sweet pepper

1 courgette

12 cherry tomatoes

12 button mushrooms

Basil leaves

Extras!
You can also cook the skewer. To do this, soak the skewers in cold water for 30 minutes before you add the vegetables to stop them burning, then brush them with a little olive oil. Get a grown-up to cook them under the grill or on the barbecue. They should be cooked when they are starting to blacken at the edges.

1 Cut the peppers in half and scrape out the seeds and white parts with a spoon. Slice them into 3cm/1in squares. Then chop the courgette into 2cm/1in chunks.

2 Take a skewer and push some vegetables on it, alternating between the different types. Do this with the other skewers until all the vegetables have been used up.

Homemade Mushrooms

Feeds 2

This is one time it's okay to play with your food! These look like the red, white-spotted wild mushrooms or toadstools you see in picture books.

You'll need:
A serrated plastic knife
A chopping board
A spoon
Scissors

Ingredients

4 cold hard-boiled eggs

2 medium tomatoes

3 tablespoons cream cheese

2 boxes cress

1 First peel the eggs by tapping them on the chopping board until they are cracked all over and then carefully peel off the shells. Slice the tomatoes in half and scoop out the seeds with a spoon.

2 Put a small dot of cream cheese inside the tomato and then stick it on top of the egg and then put a dot on the bottom of the egg and stick it to the plate. Do the same with the other eggs and then put little dots of cream cheese all over the tomatoes to make the spots.

3 With the help of a grown-up, chop the cress with the scissors and arrange it around the plate so it looks as if the mushrooms are growing in the grass.

Burger Faces

Makes 4

Cheer up boring burgers with these funny faces!

You'll need:
A large mixing bowl
A wooden spoon
A baking tray
A plastic serrated knife
A chopping board

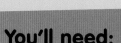

Ingredients

For the burgers:
500g/1lb 2oz minced
    beef
1 small onion, finely
    chopped
50g/2oz fresh breadcrumbs
2 free-range eggs, beaten
1 tablespoon Worcestershire
    sauce
1 tablespoon tomato
    ketchup
Oil for greasing
2 burger buns

To decorate:
Iceberg lettuce leaves
Cherry tomatoes, halved
Slices of gherkin, slice of cheese
1 tube processed cheese spread
A few black peppercorns

1 Preheat the oven 200°C/400°F/Gas mark 6. Put all of the ingredients for the burgers in a mixing bowl and mix well. Oil the baking tray.

2 With wet hands, divide the mixture into 4, then flatten into patties and place on the oiled baking sheet.

3 Get a grown-up to bake them for 12 to 15 minutes. The patties should be turned over halfway through cooking.

4 Check the centre of one burger to make sure it's cooked through; it shouldn't be red in the centre. Transfer the cooked burgers to kitchen paper to absorb the fat.

5 Put a lettuce leaf on one half of a burger bun, then place a burger on top.

6 Now comes the fun bit – decorating the burger. You can do whatever you like. Be creative!

To make burgers like those in the picture, put half a cherry tomato in the centre of the burgers for a nose, then squeeze 2 blobs of processed cheese on each for the eyes, and draw on a mouth. Squash a thin slice of gherkin above the eyes and then put a peppercorn in the centre of each face. Don't eat the peppercorns though – they're hot!

Extras!
Make them for your friends and family and let them decorate their own burgers.

You can use other foods to decorate your faces, such as beetroot, olives, mushrooms, ham, tomato ketchup, sweetcorn, and so on.

Pasta Spirals and Stars

Feeds 4

This is a great dish to make, because you get to be head chef and tell a grown-up what to do!

You'll need:

A plastic serrated knife
A chopping board
A vegetable peeler
A small star-shaped
  cookie cutter
2 large saucepans
A colander
An apron
A wooden spoon

Ingredients

1 large sweet potato
1 large courgette
100g/4oz mangetout
1 small head of broccoli
2 tomatoes
1 clove of garlic
50g/2oz beansprouts
2 teaspoons salt
250g/9oz dried pasta
  spirals (fusilli)
3 tablespoons
  olive oil

1 First peel the sweet potato and get a grown-up to slice it lengthways into 5mm/$\frac{1}{4}$in slices. Then get your cookie-cutter and cut the slices into star shapes on the chopping board. Chop the courgette into 1cm/$\frac{1}{2}$in chunks. Slice the mangetout in half and break the broccoli into florets (those are the individual flowery bits).

2 Peel and finely chop the garlic and cut the tomatoes in half. Scoop out the seeds and chop into little pieces. Get a grown-up to fill the saucepans with water, add a teaspoon of salt to each, and then bring to the boil. Be careful not to touch them as boiling water is very dangerous!

3 Now you get to boss the grown-up about! Get them to cook the pasta for you in one of the pans and then drain it in the colander.

4 Next, get them to add the sweet potato stars to the other pan of water and boil them for 5 minutes. Then get them to add them the mangetout, courgette and broccoli to the water cook for another 3 minutes and then drain the vegetables and add them to the pasta.

5 Put on your apron and get a grown-up help you with the last bit. Take one of the pans and heat the oil over a medium heat. Add the garlic and tomatoes and fry for 2 minutes or until the tomatoes soften, then throw in the beansprouts, stir them around for a minute, and add all the pasta and vegetables. Keep stirring until everything has mixed together and it's all hot. To serve, divide the mixture between 4 plates.

Extras!

You can use lots of different vegetables in this pasta, try boiling pieces of carrot, French beans, or peas, or frying thinly sliced sweet peppers, mushrooms and onions.

Fisherman's Pie

Feeds 4-6

This tasty meal really is the catch of the day!

You'll need:
A whisk
A mixing bowl
A potato peeler
A large saucepan
A potato masher
A citrus juicer
A plastic serrated knife
A large ovenproof dish

Ingredients

1.25kg/2^1/2lb potatoes
50g/2oz butter
100g/4oz low-fat soft cheese
500ml/18fl oz low-fat
   whipping cream
1 lemon
1 teaspoon salt
^{1}/2 teaspoon black
   pepper
5 tablespoons chopped
   flat-leaved parsley
10oz smoked white fish
10oz large cooked prawns
2 courgettes, chopped into chunks
50g/2oz sweetcorn kernels
50g/2oz Cheddar cheese

1 Preheat the oven to:
200°C/400°F/Gas mark 6.

2 Peel the potatoes and cut them into chunks. Get a grown-up to boil them in a pan of water for 15 minutes and drain them for you. When they've cooled down, mash them, add the butter and mash them again.

3 Next, make the sauce by whisking together the low-fat soft cheese and the low-fat whipping cream until smooth. Grate the lemon rind and squeeze the juice. Stir both into the sauce and sprinkle with salt, pepper and parsley. Add 4 tablespoons of the mashed potatoes to the sauce to thicken it.

4 Slice the fish into big pieces and add to the sauce with the courgettes, prawns and sweetcorn. Pour into an ovenproof dish.

5 Cover the fish and sauce with the mashed potato, starting from the edges and working your way into the centre. Roughen the surface with a fork so it becomes nice and crisp.

6 Grate the Cheddar cheese over the pie and ask a grown-up to bake it in the oven for 35 to 40 minutes, or until the top is golden-brown. You can serve the pie with garden peas and green vegetables or even baked beans.

Extras!

In the picture, we've left out the middle, so you can see the inside, but make sure you follow the recipe and cover the top. If you have a piping bag use that, it will make the mashed potato look more professional. You can also use a mixture of oily fish such as salmon and trout. You can also add 4 hard-boiled eggs, sliced into quarters.

Goldfish and Fries

Feeds 4

You'll need:
A vegetable peeler
A plastic serrated knife
A saucepan
A potato masher
A mixing bowl
A fork
3 shallow bowls
A frying pan
A roasting tin

Ingredients

For the goldfish cakes:
250g/9oz potatoes
25g/1oz butter
250g/9oz white fish (cod,
   haddock, coley, etc.)
1 tablespoon chopped parsley
Salt and black pepper
3 tablespoons plain flour
1 free-range egg, beaten
75g/3oz fresh breadcrumbs
Olive oil

For the French fries:
4 large potatoes
1-2 tablespoons sunflower oil

1 To make the goldfish cakes, peel the potatoes with the vegetable peeler, being careful with the sharp edge, then chop them into large chunks. Ask a grown-up to put the potatoes in the saucepan with enough water to cover, and to boil the potatoes for 15 minutes, then drain them. When they have cooled down, mash them with the masher, then add the butter and mash them again.

2 Next, ask a grown-up to put the fish in a saucepan of boiling water and simmer it for 8 minutes (simmer means cook it on a low heat so it's just bubbling). After it's cooked, get the grown-up to remove the fish from the pan, put it on a plate and, when it has cooled, flake it into chunks, and take out any bones that are left. This is often done with tweezers.

3 Mix the potato and fish in a mixing bowl, add the parsley and a pinch of salt and pepper, and mix it all together.

4 Wet your hands and divide the mixture into 4, and then mould each piece into a fish shape. When they are finished, refrigerate them for 20 to 30 minutes to firm up.

5 Now take 3 small, shallow bowls and put the flour in one, the egg in the next and the breadcrumbs in the last. To coat the fish, first roll them in the flour, tapping off the excess, then coat in the egg, and finally coat in the bread-crumbs, pressing the crumbs on firmly so they stick.

6 Now ask a grown-up to shallow -fry them for you in olive oil for 4 to 5 minutes on each side, or until they are golden-brown.

7 To make the French fries, preheat the oven to 220°C/425°F/Gas mark 7. Peel the potatoes with the vegetable peeler, and slice them, into long pieces about 1cm/^{1}/2in wide. Put them in a roasting tin and pour the oil over the French fries and mix them around so they are coated.

8 Ask a grown-up to cook them in the oven for 15 minutes, giving them a shake halfway through, until they are golden-brown.

Extras!
Trying adding 4 finely chopped spring onions or 4 rashers chopped cooked bacon to the potato mixture. Also try making the French fries from sweet potatoes or pumpkin.

Pasta Bake

Feeds 4

This is really good dish to warm you up on a cold winter's night.

You'll need:
A plastic serrated knife
2 large saucepans
A colander
A cheese grater
A large ovenproof dish

Ingredients

350g/13oz dried pasta shapes (the ones in the picture are called penne)

1 head broccoli

125g/4oz cooked ham, chopped

1 x 400g/14oz tin chopped plum tomatoes

2 tsp dried oregano

Salt and black pepper

125/4oz Cheddar or mozzarella cheese

1 Preheat the oven to: 200°C/400°F/Gas mark 6.

2 Chop the broccoli into florets (small flowery bits). Then get a grown-up to fill the 2 saucepans with water and to bring them to the boil. Tell them to cook the broccoli for 5 minutes in one of the saucepans and then to cook the pasta for as long as it says on the packet in the other one.

3 When they are cooked, ask the grown-up to drain the vegetables in the colander.

4 When they've cooled down a little, pour the pasta and broccoli into a large ovenproof dish and add the ham, tomatoes, oregano, and a pinch of salt and pepper. Give everything a good stir so it's all mixed up, then grate the cheese and sprinkle all over the top.

5 Get a grown-up to bake it in the middle of the oven for 20 to 25 minutes or until it's bubbling and golden on top.

Extras!

Try swapping the broccoli for different vegetables such as courgettes, sweet peppers, French beans or mushrooms, and change the ham for bacon, tuna or cooked chicken.

Use different pasta shapes, you can get some really cool ones!

Rice and Peas

Feeds 4

This is a simple but tasty dish that is great for vegetarians.

You'll need:

A large saucepan
A colander
A large mixing bowl
A juicer

Ingredients

175g/6oz rice

225g/8oz frozen peas

1 x 410g/14oz can of chick-peas, drained

5 tablespoons olive oil

1 lemon, juice squeezed

Salt and black pepper

1 Get a grown-up to cook the rice for you for as long as it says on the packet. Tell them to add the peas to the rice 4 to 5 minutes before it's ready. When the rice and peas are cooked, put them in a colander or sieve and rinse them under plenty of cold running water until they are cold.

2 Now put the rice, peas and chick-peas in a mixing bowl.

3 Squeeze the juice from the lemon with a juicer and pour it into the bowl with the olive oil. Add a pinch of salt and a pinch of black pepper and give everything a really good stir.

Extras!

Try adding different vegetables such as chopped sweet pepper, sweetcorn, Spanish onion or mushrooms. You can also swap the chick-peas for the same amount of cooked black-eyed peas or other beans.

Spanish Tortilla

Feeds 4

A Spanish tortilla is a simple recipe for you to cook for the family. It is actually an omelette but in Spain they call it a tortilla, although it is nothing like the Mexican tortillas.

You'll need:
A serrated plastic knife
A chopping board
A spoon
A mixing bowl
A fork
A large frying pan
A fish slice
Oven gloves
An apron

Ingredients

1 onion

1 red sweet pepper

250g/9oz cooked potatoes

8 eggs

Salt and pepper

2 tablespoons olive oil

1 Carefully peel and finely chop the onion, using the plastic knife on a chopping board. Then cut the sweet pepper in half and scrape out the seeds and white parts with a spoon. Then chop it into small squares.

2 Next, chop the potato into chunks leaving the skin on. Break the eggs into a bowl, add a pinch of salt and pepper, and beat them with a fork. You'll need to get a grown-up to help you cook the omelette and you'll need to wear oven gloves and an apron.

3 Preheat the grill to high. Pour the oil into the frying pan and heat it over a medium heat. Add the onion and peppers and fry them for 5 minutes, stirring them with the fish slice. Be careful of the hot frying pan! Add the potatoes and fry for another 2 minutes.

4 Pour the egg mixture over the contents of the frying pan. Stir, then reduce the heat to low and leave the omelette to cook for 4 to 5 minutes, or until the underside is cooked but the top is still a bit runny. Now carefully put the frying pan under the grill for 2 minutes, or until the omelette is puffy and golden.

5 Cut the omelette into 4 pieces, using the fish slice, and transfer it to 4 plates. Spanish omelette goes really well with salad.

Extras!

Try adding 1 or 2 of the following: 3 tablespoons grated cheese or chopped ham to the egg mixture, 100g/4oz chopped Spanish sausage (chorizo) when you cook the onions, or 2 chopped tomatoes when you cook the potatoes.

Pizza-making Fun for the Family

Makes 4 pizzas

If you're cooking for the family or have friends over, make the dough yourself and let everyone have fun adding their own toppings.

You'll need:
A food processor
1 large mixing bowl
1 rolling pin
4 baking trays (if you want to cook all of them at once)

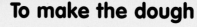

Dough:
650g/1lb 7oz strong flour or Italian Tipo 'OO' flour
1 x 7g/^{1}/4oz sachets of dried yeast
2 teaspoons salt
1 teaspoon sugar
350ml/9 fl oz warm water

Tomato topping:
1 x 400g/14oz can chopped tomatoes
2 garlic cloves, finely chopped
1 tablespoon dried oregano
1 teaspoon sugar
3 tablespoon olive oil

To make the dough

1 Put the flour, yeast, salt and sugar together in a food processor. Get a grown-up to help you with this.

2 Turn to a medium speed and start to slowly pour in the water until all of it has been added. When the mixture forms a big ball, dust a work surface with flour and tip the dough on to it.

3 Now for the fun bit – kneading! Basically, you've got to push, roll, stretch and fold the dough over and over again until it feels smooth and stretchy. This will take about 3 to 5 minutes.

4 Now put your dough in a clean bowl and cover it with a damp tea towel. Leave for about 1 to 1^{1}/2 hours or until it has doubled in size.

5 Turn the oven on as hot as it goes and then start making the tomato topping. Put the tomatoes, garlic, oregano, sugar and oil in a bowl and mash them with a fork until they're mushy.

6 Now take your dough and give it a punch in the middle to knock the air out of it. Then cut into 4 pieces. Roll each piece into squares or circles 0.5cm/^{1}/4in thick and place on a floured baking tray. Spread 2 to 3 tablespoons of topping over each pizza, leaving a space around the edge for the crust and then add your toppings.

Toppings

Everyone likes different things on their pizzas. Here are some ideas to get you started.

Oh, and remember that in Italy, where pizza comes from, they don't use too much topping because they make the pizza go soggy and then it doesn't taste as good!

Cheese: cubes of fresh mozzarella (it goes stringy when it's cooked) or grated Cheddar.
Meat: ham, pepperoni, chicken, grilled or fried bacon.
Vegetables: red peppers, mushrooms, olives, tomatoes, courgettes, spinach.

Ask a grown-up to bake your pizzas in the oven for 7 to 10 minutes, or until the crust is golden and the cheese has melted.

Fajitas

Feeds 4

You'll need:
A serrated plastic knife
A spoon
A chopping board
A mixing bowl
A roasting tin

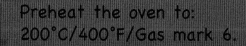

Ingredients

1 red onion

1 sweet red pepper

1 sweet yellow pepper

4 skinless chicken breasts

3 tablespoons olive oil

1 lime, juice squeezed

1 teaspoon ground cumin

1 teaspoon smoked paprika

1 teaspoon oregano

1 avocado

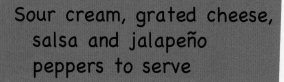

8 x 25cm/10in soft
  (flour) tortillas

Sour cream, grated cheese,
  salsa and jalapeño
  peppers to serve

1 Preheat the oven to:
200°C/400°F/Gas mark 6.

2 Cut peppers in half and scrape out
the seeds and white parts with a
spoon, and slice into strips. Peel
the onion and slice that too. Next
cut the chicken into 1cm/^{1}/2in
strips the put it in the bowl with
the onions.

3 Mix the oil, lime juice, cumin,
paprika and oregano in a bowl, pour
this over the chicken and vegetables
and mix together until everything
is coated.

4 Pour the mixture into a roasting
tin and get a grown-up to put it
the oven for 12 minutes. Get the
grown-up to give the tin a shake
halfway through. While everything
is in the oven, peel and chop the
avocado. A really easy way to do
this it to cut round the middle
from top to bottom, take out the
stone, and then put the edge of a
big spoon between the skin and the
flesh and scoop it out.

5 When the chicken is cooked, it will no longer be pink in the middle. Get a grown-up to put it on a plate, and put it on the table with the avocado, tortillas and everything else.

6 Get everyone to make their own fajitas, put a bit of everything on a tortilla and rolling it up.

Extras!
Try adding other vegetables to your fajitas, such as a sliced courgette and some sliced mushrooms. Or why not try sprinkling a tablespoon or 2 of chopped coriander leaves over the chicken and vegetables before serving for a fresh, herby taste?

Pretty Potato Cakes

Makes 4

These are a fun way of making a potato side-dish.

You'll need:
A vegetable peeler
A cheese grater
A mixing bowl
A baking tray
A fish slice

Ingredients

4 large potatoes

1 free-range egg, beaten

75g/3oz butter, melted

To decorate:

Slices of radish or cherry tomatoes; and sweet red pepper

Extras!
Try replacing half the potato with mashed pumpkin, sweet potato or parsnip.

1 Preheat the oven to: 220°C/425°F/Gas 7.

2 With a grown-up, peel the potatoes with the vegetable peeler and then coarsely grate them with the cheese grater. Be careful with the sharp bits of the peeler and grater!

3 Put the grated potato in a mixing bowl and pour the beaten egg and the melted butter over it. Mix everything together so it's well coated, and then divide the mixture into 4. Squash each portion into a flat cake on the baking tray.

4 Get a grown-up to put the potato cakes in the oven and bake them for 15 minutes. Then get them to carefully turn them over and put them back in the oven for another 10 to 15 minutes, or until they are crisp and golden.

5 Get the grown-up to take them out of the oven and put them on the plates. Then you can make faces on them with slices of radish or cherry tomato for the eyes and a slice of sweet red pepper or tomato for the mouth.

Greek Salad

This is a quick and tasty salad recipe, which is eaten all over Greece.

You'll need:
A serrated plastic knife
A chopping board
A large mixing bowl
A jam jar (with lid)

Ingredients

For the salad:
1 iceberg lettuce
6 tomatoes
1 medium cucumber
200g/8oz feta
  cheese
16 stoned black olives,
  halved

For the dressing:
3 tablespoons olive oil
1 tablespoon lemon juice
1 teaspoon Dijon-style mustard
1 teaspoon oregano
A pinch black pepper

1 First slice the lettuce, then chop the tomatoes, cucumber and feta into big chunks and put them all in a large bowl with the olives.

2 To make the dressing, put the olive oil, lemon juice, mustard, oregano and a pinch of pepper in a jam jar, and screw on the lid tightly.

3 When you're ready to serve the salad, shake the dressing in the jar until it's all mixed up, then pour it over the salad and toss everything lightly so the salad is coated with the dressing.

4 Bring it to the table and let everyone help themselves.

Extras!
Try adding half a sliced red onion or 2 tablespoons fresh chopped parsley or mint leaves to your salad.

Chicken Skewers

Feeds 4

Impress your family by making these delicious kebabs.

You'll need:
A plastic serrated knife
A chopping board
A juicer
Some skewers soaked in
   cold water

Ingredients

1 red onion

2 red pepper

4 skinless chicken
   breasts

150ml/5fl oz olive oil

1 teaspoon paprika

2 garlic cloves, finely
   chopped

1 lime, juice squeezed

1 Carefully peel the onion with a plastic knife and chop into 2.5cm/1in chunks, then cut the pepper in half and scrape out the seeds and white parts with a spoon. Chop into pieces the same size as the onion, then do the same with the chicken.

2 Mix the oil, paprika, garlic and lime juice together in a bowl and stir in the chicken. Put them into the refrigerator for 1 hour to marinate, and let the flavours combine.

3 When you ready to cook the skewers, push alternate pieces of chicken and vegetable on to the skewers until they are used up.

4 Get a grown-up to cook the skewers under a hot grill or on the barbecue for 7 to 10 minutes. Check to see if they are cooked inside by cutting the thickest piece of chicken, there shouldn't be any pink inside.

Extras!
Try adding courgette, mushrooms and cherry tomatoes,
and add extra herbs and spices to the marinade such
as oregano or cumin.

Tomato Soup

Feeds 4

You'll need:
An apron
A plastic serrated knife
A chopping board
A large saucepan
A blender

Ingredients

1 large onion

1 tablespoon olive oil

1 x 400g/14oz tin plum
    tomatoes, chopped

1 tablespoon tomato purée

A bunch of basil leaves

550ml/1pt vegetable
    stock

1/2 teaspoon salt

1/2 teaspoon black pepper

Basil leaves to decorate

1 Wearing an apron, first peel and thinly slice the onion. Then get a grown-up to help you with the cooking. The saucepan and soup will be very hot, so never try this on your own.

2 Put the oil and the onion in the saucepan, stir them, and then cook on a low heat for 10 minutes or until the onions are soft.

3 Add the rest of the ingredients and simmer (that means cook so it's barely bubbling) for 30 minutes, stirring from time to time.

4 Let the mixture cool down a bit and then get a grown-up to help with the next part. Carefully pour the mixture into the blender, put on the lid and hold it down. Blend until the mixture is really smooth, then pour it back into the saucepan. Warm it up just until it's hot and serve it with some nice crusty bread. Decorate with a few basil leaves.

Extras!
Try stirring 3 tablespoons of single or double cream into the soup when you warm it up at the end. This will make it cream of tomato soup.

Mixed Green Salad with Chicken and Bacon

Feeds 4

This is a great dish for all the family.

You'll need:

A chopping board
A plastic serrated
knife
A large mixing bowl
A jam jar (with lid)

Ingredients

For the salad:

1 small lettuce

1 cucumber

6 tomatoes

$1/2$ Spanish onion

1 sweet pepper

2 cooked chicken breasts

8 rashers of grilled
or fried bacon

For the dressing:

5 tablespoon olive oil

2 tablespoon fresh
lemon juice

2 tablespoon Dijon mustard

1 tablespoon runny honey

1 Take a chopping board and chop all of the ingredients into pieces that are all the same size. Put them all into a mixing bowl.

2 To make the dressing, put the dressing ingredients into the jam jar and screw the lid on tightly.

3 When you are ready to eat the salad, give the dressing a really good shake so it's all mixed up, then pour it over the salad. Give it all a good mix so everything is coated in the dressing, then take it to the table and let everyone serve themselves.

Extras!

Try using different types of vegetables or salad leaves in your salad, such as courgettes, spring onions, rocket and watercress. You can exchange the chicken and bacon for cubes of cheese, ham or tuna. Experiment and see which one you like best.

Bread & Butter Pudding

Serves 6

You'll need:

A mixing bowl
A butter knife
A whisk
An ovenproof dish
  or pie dish
Oven gloves

Ingredients

75g/3oz sultanas

75g/3oz raisins

12 slices white bread,
  crusts removed

100g/4oz unsalted
  butter, softened

4 free-range eggs, beaten

100g/4oz caster sugar

2 teaspoons vanilla
  essence

550ml/1pt milk

275ml/10fl oz double cream

1 teaspoon powdered cinnamon

2 tablespoons brown sugar

1 Preheat the oven to:
180°C/350°F/Gas mark 4.

2 Scatter half of the sultanas and raisins over the bottom of the ovenproof dish. Then butter the slices of bread on one side and cut them half.

3 Combine the beaten eggs with the sugar, milk, cream and vanilla and beat well.

4 Next, arrange the bread slices over the bottom of the ovenproof dish, so they overlap. Scatter the rest of the fruit over them and pour the creamy mixture all over the bread.

5 Sprinkle with cinnamon and brown sugar and get a grown-up to put the pudding in the middle of the oven. Bake for 30 to 40 minutes, or until top is golden-brown.

6 Wear oven gloves to take the pudding to the table and let each person serve themselves with a big spoon.

Extras!

Try using orange marmalade or peanut butter instead of unsalted butter. Or use chocolate chips instead of the sultanas.

Fruit Salad

Healthy and fun to make, you can choose your favourite fruits.

You'll need:
A plastic serrated knife
A chopping board

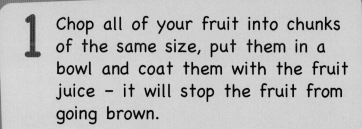

Ingredients

125ml/4fl oz apple or
  orange juice
2 tablespoons runny honey
250ml/9fl oz plain yogurt

Try using some of these:
Apples
Berries
Grapes
Strawberries
Kiwi fruits
Different types
  of melon
Mangoes
Oranges
Pears
Plums

1 Chop all of your fruit into chunks of the same size, put them in a bowl and coat them with the fruit juice – it will stop the fruit from going brown.

2 Mix the honey with the yogurt and pour it over the top.

Extras!
Try sprinkling with chopped nuts or chopped dried fruits.

Halloween Pumpkin Soup

Feeds 6-8

This is a really cool soup to make for a Halloween party. Serve it in a pumpkin head.

You'll need:
A large saucepan
An apron
A serrated knife
A chopping board

Ingredients

1 large pumpkin (1.5kg/3lb), to produce about 750g/$1^1/2$lb of flesh

2 tablespoon olive oil

1 large onion, chopped

2 garlic cloves, finely chopped

2 teaspoons ground cumin

2 teaspoons paprika

1 tablespoon ground coriander

550ml/1pt vegetable stock

550ml/1pt milk

1 teaspoon salt

$^1/2$ teaspoon black pepper

1 First ask a grown-up to help you hollow out the pumpkin. Ask them to cut a large hole in the top for you, then scrape out the seeds and throw them away (or dry them, sprinkle with a little salt and eat them later). Now scrape out the orange flesh, being careful not to break through the skin of the pumpkin.

2 Put on your apron and get a grown-up to help you with the cooking. The saucepan and soup will be very hot, so never try this by yourself.

3 Heat the oil in the saucepan, and add the onion and garlic. Stir well. Reduce the heat and cook on a low heat for 10 minutes, or until the onions are soft.

4 Add the spices and stir for 2 to 3 minutes before adding the rest of the ingredients, including the pumpkin flesh. Simmer (that means cook so it's barely bubbling) for 30 minutes, stirring from time to time.

5 Let the mixture cool down for about 20 minutes, then get a grown-up help with the next part. Carefully pour the mixture into the blender, put on the lid and hold it down, covered with a tea towel. Whiz it up until it's really smooth; there's lots of soup so you may have to do this is in 2 or 3 batches.

6 Pour the liquid back into the saucepan, warm it up and serve it with some garlic bread to scare off the vampires!

Extras!
To serve it in a pumpkin head, draw a scary face on the pumpkin with a magic marker. Put the head in an oven preheated to 150°C/300°F/Gas mark 2 for 10 to 15 minutes to warm it up, before pouring your soup inside. Sprinkle the soup with lots of chopped parsley before serving. Make some garlic toast, and cut it into interesting shapes, such as stars and moons, using a cookie cutter.

Easter Bunny Cookies

Makes 16-20

You'll need:

A mixing bowl
A wooden spoon
A rabbit-shaped
  cookie cutter
A palette knife
A baking tray
A wire cooling rack

Ingredients

350g/12oz self-raising
  flour

A pinch of salt

200g/8oz butter,
  chilled, cut in cubes

100g/4oz caster sugar

Decoration:

Chocolate chips or
  green ball sprinkles
  for the eyes

1 Preheat the oven to 200°C/ 400°F/ Gas mark 6. Put the flour, salt and butter in a mixing bowl and rub it together with your fingertips until it looks like breadcrumbs.

2 Add the sugar and stir the mixture until it forms a dough.

3 Dust a work surface and rolling pin with a little flour and roll out the dough until it is 1cm/^{1}/2in thick.

4 Grease the baking tray with a little butter, then cut out bunny shapes with the cookie cutter and transfer them to the tray using the palette knife. Put a chocolate or green ball on each cookie for an eye.

5 Ask a grown-up to bake them in the oven for 15 to 20 minutes or until golden. Then ask the grown-up to arrange them on a wire cooling rack, and leave them to cool.

Ice Cream Clowns

Make 8

You'll need:
An ice-cream scoop
8 paper cup-cake cases

Ingredients

A tub of ice-cream
 your favourite flavour

8 ice-cream cones

2 packets of
 Smarties or M&Ms

1 Make these 2 at a time or the ice-cream will melt. Take a scoop of ice-cream and put it in a cup-cake case. Quickly make a face in the ice-cream by pushing the Smarties or M&Ms into the front. Push on an ice-cream cone and put them in the freezer.

2 Do the same with the rest and they'll be ready for your party.

Fruit Skewers

You can use any mix of fruit for these skewers, start with you favourites and then try different ones you've never had before.

You'll need:
A plastic serrated knife
A chopping board
Some wooden skewers

Ingredients

Try using some of these:

Apple

Grapes

Cherries

Different
 types of melon

Mango

Pear

1 All you have to do it chop up the fruit into bite-size chunks. Scrape out seeds and cut of the hard skin from fruit like melon or mango.

2 Now push the chunks on to the skewers, one fruit after the other so they look colourful and pretty.

Note:
If you're using apple or pear, put them in a bowl and sprinkle with a little orange juice to stop them turning brown.

Mini Burgers

Makes 4

You'll need:
A large mixing bowl
A wooden spoon
A baking tray
A plastic serrated knife
A chopping board
12 cocktail sticks

Ingredients

A little olive oil
Tomato ketchup
12 hamburger buns
6 slices of Swiss cheese
   cut into quarters
3 small tomatoes, sliced

For the patties:
500g/1lb 2oz minced
   beef
1 small onion, finely chopped
50g/2oz fresh breadcrumbs
2 free-range eggs, beaten
1 tablespoon
   Worcestershire sauce
1 tablespoon
   tomato ketchup

1 Preheat the oven to 200°C/ 400°F/ Gas mark 6. Put all the ingredients for the patties in a mixing bowl and mix well. Grease the baking tray with the olive oil.

2 With wet hands, divide the mixture into 12 balls, then flatten it into little patties and place on the oiled tray.

3 Get a grown-up to cook them for 10 to 12 minutes, turning them over halfway through the cooking. While they are cooking, get the buns ready. Spread some ketchup on the bottom half of each bun and then put on a slice of cheese on it.

4 When the burgers are cooked, check the middle of one of them to make sure it's not pink. Put a hamburger on the slice of cheese and top with another slice of cheese. Then add a slice of tomato. Cover with the top of the bun.

5 Push a cocktail stick through the middle so the contents don't fall out, but remember to remove it before serving.

Birthday Cake

Celebrating a birthday in the family with a homemade cake is far more personal and special than a shop-bought one.

You'll need:
2 x 18cm/7in
  sandwich tins
Scissors
Some non-stick
  baking paper
A large mixing bowl
A wooden
spoon
A palette
knife
A skewer
A wire cooling rack

Birthday candles,
as many as the
person's age.

Ingredients

175g/6oz softened butter
175g/6oz caster sugar
3 medium free-range eggs
1 teaspoon vanilla essence
175g/6oz self-raising flour
1 teaspoon baking powder

For decoration:
5-6 tablespoons apricot jam
75g/3oz unsalted butter
175g/6oz icing sugar
3 drops vanilla essence
Sprinkles or other cake decorations

1 First grease and line the sandwich tins. Place 1 tin on 2 sheets of non-stick baking paper and draw round it, then cut out the circles. Grease the inside of the tins with butter and then put the paper circles in the bottom.

2 Preheat the oven to 190°C/ 375°F/ Gas mark 5. Put the sugar and butter in a mixing bowl and beat together until creamy. Add the eggs and vanilla essence and beat again until the mixture is smooth.

3 Sift the flour into a bowl. Then add it into the mixture and mix well.

4 Divide the mixture between the 2 tins and smooth the top with a palette knife. Ask a grown-up to bake them in the middle of the oven for about 20 minutes, or until risen and in golden on top. Test to see if the cake is done by pushing a wooden skewer in the middle of the cakes. If it comes out clean then they're ready.

5 Leave the cakes to cool for 5 minutes then take them out of their tins and put them on to the wire rack. When they are completely cool, ask a grown-up to slice them into 3 layers across the centre with a sharp knife.

6 Spread 2 tablespoons apricot jam on 3 of the slices of cake. Arrange them on top of each other, with the layer without jam on the top.

7 To make the icing, put the butter and icing sugar into a bowl and beat until creamy. Add the vanilla essence and 1 tablespoon water. Beat until the mixture is smooth, thick and spreadable. If it's too thick, add another tablespoon of water.

8 Spread the icing all over the cake with a palette knife and then add sprinkles or other cake decorations.

Extras!

For a chocolate cake, add 2 tablespoons unsweetened cocoa powder to the flour. For the icing, add 1 tablespoon unsweetened cocoa powder and an extra tablespoon of water to the mixture.

Bat Cookies

Makes 10-12

These cool cookies are just right for a Halloween party!

You'll need:
A large mixing bowl
A small bowl
A sieve
A wooden spoon
A rolling pin
A piping bag or a small plastic
   freezer bag
A chopping board
A wire cooling rack
A baking tray or
Swiss roll tin (a flat
   baking sheet with a 5cm/2in rim)
A bat-shaped cookie cutter

Ingredients

For the cookies:
100g/4oz caster sugar
100g/4oz softened butter,
   plus more for greasing
   the tray
1 free-range egg, beaten
2 drops vanilla essence
225g/8oz plain flour, plus
   more for dusting

For the icing:
200g/7oz icing sugar
Black food colouring
Orange food colouring

1 Preheat the oven to 190°C/ 375°F/ Gas mark 5. Put the sugar and butter in a large mixing bowl and beat together until creamy.

2 Add the egg and vanilla essence and keep beating until the mixture is smooth. Now stir in the flour, a little at a time, until you have a smooth dough.

3 Dust the chopping board and rolling pin with a little flour and roll the dough out until it's about 5mm/$\frac{1}{4}$in thick; dust with more flour if it sticks to the board.

4 Butter a baking tray or Swiss roll tin. Then use a cookie cutter to cut out the cookies. Put the cookies on the baking tray or Swiss roll tin. If there are bits left over, bake them too, and you can eat them later as a treat for your hard work!

5 Get a grown-up to put the baking tray or Swiss roll tin in the middle of the oven and bake for 10 minutes. When ready, get the grown-up to transfer them to a wire rack to cool.

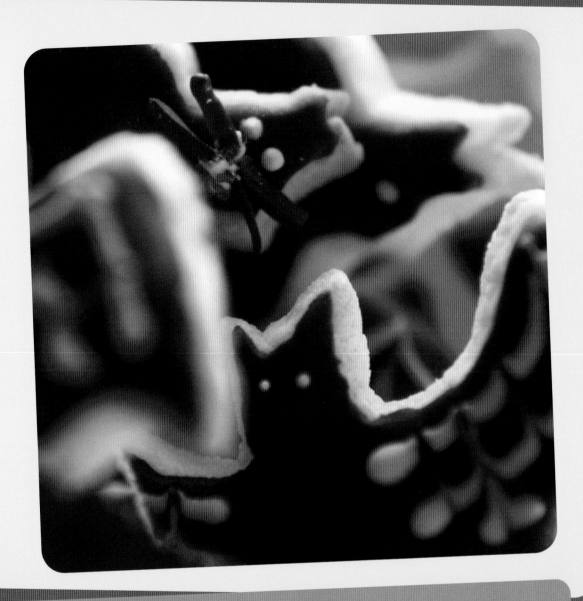

6 To make the icing, sift the icing sugar into a bowl and add a tablespoon of water. Mix with a wooden or a plastic spoon.

7 Take 3 tablespoons of the icing and put in it a small bowl. Add a few drops of orange food colouring to make it bright orange. Add black food colouring to the rest of the icing.

8 Spread the black icing over the cookies with a palette knife. Put the orange icing in a piping bag or a freezer bag with the corner snipped off. Draw lines down the wings and make little dots for eyes.

Extras!

You can easily use the same cookie mixture for Christmas cookies. Use a Christmas tree cookie cutter to get the right shape and spread the cookie with green icing. Dot with white icing for the tree decorations.

Spider Web Cakes

Makes 16

Perfect cakes for Halloween!

You'll need:
A large mixing bowl
A wooden spoon
Sieve
A 16 cup-cake tray
   or 16 paper-cake cases
A wire cooling rack
Plastic freezer bag
A cocktail stick

Ingredients

100g/4oz caster sugar
100g/4oz butter,
   softened
2 free-range eggs, beaten
100g/4oz self-raising
   flour
50g/2oz sultanas

For the icing:
150g/5oz icing sugar
A few drops of brown
   food colouring

1 Preheat the oven 190°C/375°F/Gas 5. Put the sugar and butter in a mixing bowl and beat until they are creamy. Now add the eggs and beat again until the mixture is smooth.

2 Next sift the flour into a bowl. This gets air into the flour and makes the cakes fluffier. When all the flour is in the bowl, stir it into the mixture and then mix in the sultanas. They are the dead flies in your spider web cakes!

3 Divide the mixture between the cups in the baking tray or the cake-cases and ask a grown-up to bake them in the oven for 15 to 20 minutes, or until they've risen and are golden. Then ask the grown-up to put them on a wire rack to cool.

4 Meanwhile, make the icing. Sift the icing sugar into a small bowl and add 1 tablespoon of water. Mix it together until it forms a thick smooth paste, adding a little more water if you need to. Take 4 tablespoons of the icing and put it in another bowl.

5 Mix in the food colouring, a few drops at a time, until the icing is dark brown.

6 When the cakes are cool, spread the white icing over the tops of the cakes. Now take a plastic freezer bag and cut the tip of one corner. Spoon in the brown icing and then draw circles on the tops of the cakes, starting small and making bigger and bigger circles until you reach the edge.

7 When you have covered all the cakes, take a cocktail stick and pull in through the circles from the inside to the edge, about 6 or 7 times on each cake, so it looks like a spider's web.

Extras!

You can swap the sultanas for the same amount of chocolate chips if you like. You can also try using different food colourings and draw pictures or names on top of your cakes.

Choc-nut Apples

Makes 8

Just like the ones you get at the fairground. Great fun for the guests if you are giving a party!

You'll need:
A microwave
8 wooden lollypop
  sticks
A mixing bowl

Ingredients

8 small red apples

200g/7oz chocolate
  (milk, white or dark,
  whichever is your
  favourite)

75g/3oz chopped nuts

Extras!
You can try rolling the chocolate apples in sweets such as sprinkles, hundreds-and-thousands or crushed M&Ms.

1 First wash the apples in a little washing-up liquid to make sure the skin is not only clean but also free of wax that would stop the chocolate from sticking to it. Make sure you rinse all the liquid off with water. Push the lollypop sticks into the end of the apples and refrigerate them until they are cold.

2 Break the chocolate into pieces. The easiest way to do this is to bang the packet on the edge of the work surface, before you open it. Put the chocolate pieces in the mixing bowl.

3 Put the bowl in the microwave oven, set to defrost, and defrost for 2 minutes or until the chocolate has melted.
If you don't have a microwave oven, get a grown-up to heat about 6cm/2in water in a large saucepan until it's steaming, then put the mixing bowl on top to melt the chocolate.

4 Now take your apples and dip them in the chocolate. You might need to use a spoon to make sure the apples are completely covered.

5 Then roll them in the chopped nuts so they stick to the chocolate. When they are completely covered, refrigerate them until chocolate has set hard.

Index